Text Copyright of Shaya Weaver, 2020

Table of Contents

Chapter 1: Gemini Personality Profile

Ruling Planet: Mercury

Symbol: the twins

Element: air

Quality: mutable

Gemini Traits: adaptable, careless, changeable, charming, chatty, clever, confident, curious, deceptive, distractible, easy going, easily bored, emotionally detached, extroverted, fickle, flirtatious, fun, funny, generous, idealistic, impulsive, Indecisive, inquisitive, intellectual, moody, open-minded, optimistic, persuasive, progressive, restless, self-absorbed, tolerant, unreliable

Adaptable

Adaptability is one of Gemini's many positive traits. Geminis rarely become mired in routines, and they have the mental flexibility required to adapt to new situations and incorporate new ideas into their worldviews.

Geminis tend to be on the cutting edge of everything, eager to learn, try out new technologies, and identify new ways of doing things.

Gemini versatility is useful for career development or just making a living, as Geminis have many different skills to fall back on and can quickly develop new ones. What they do not know, they can usually bluff their way through, and they are sufficiently flexible to adapt well to new workplaces and roles.

Because they are so adaptable, Geminis can fit into many different social groups and environments. They are good chameleons, able to tailor their conversational styles and behaviors to the requirements of different social groups. As a result, they tend to have many friends from different walks of life and establish themselves quickly when they move to new places, even when adapting to different cultures and social rules.

Geminis are so good at adapting their social strategies that they seem to be entirely different people from one social venue to the next. Most move confidently through the social world unless other aspects in their natal zodiacs incline them to be shyer than a typical Gemini.*

Gemini adaptability can support brilliant innovation because Geminis are always looking for new and more effective ways to achieve their goals or those of the organizations where they work or volunteer. Their natural adaptability drives them to question the status quo and come up with novel solutions and strategies.

Careless

Carelessness is an unfortunate aspect of the Gemini personality. Geminis are good at losing things, particularly small handheld items. They drop things without noticing or leave things at random locations and forget where they put them. As a result, they spend a lot of time running around their homes frantically searching, and they are often late for appointments.

---

* The natal zodiac refers to the positions of the planets in the sky at the time of birth. Important influences in the natal zodiac include the sun sign (the one most people know), the moon sign, and the rising sign (also known as the ascendant). Other elements in the natal zodiac can influence how the sun sign is expressed. For example, a Gemini with Virgo rising would be more practical, better organized, shyer, and more likely to hang back in social situations than a typical Gemini.

Because Geminis tend to be careless, they are also accident-prone. They leave things until the last minute and then have to rush around to catch up, and they do not pay attention to the hazards around them, which puts them at risk for all sorts of mishaps.

Geminis also spend their money carelessly, dropping everything on a fun time or spending lavishly in a fit of generosity toward others that leaves them unable to pay their bills. They tend to live in the moment and have trouble planning for the future, so they can do a lot of damage to their finances.

Geminis are equally careless when choosing friends and lovers. They leap into new romances and friendships even when there are many red flags right from the start, and they can be just as careless when exiting a romance or a friendship, leaving anger and hurt feelings in their wake.

Geminis may live in a chronic state of chaos unless they develop a more conscientious approach to life. Otherwise, they can slide into debt, suffer from illnesses or injuries caused by carelessness, and leave an unusually high number of broken romances and friendships behind them.

When the ascendant brings more balance to the personality, Gemini carelessness is significantly reduced (though this also reduces Gemini's natural spontaneity). Geminis with Taurus, Cancer, Virgo, Scorpio, or Capricorn rising tend to be more conscientious than typical Geminis.

Changeable

Geminis are highly changeable, which can be upsetting for friends and lovers who require consistency. Because they are so openminded, adaptable, and moody, Geminis change their minds, their feelings, their lifestyles, and (in some cases) even their personalities, belief systems, and preferences on a regular basis.

Geminis can be baffling to more stable individuals because what they desperately want one day may irritate or repel them the next. Their needs and desires are ever shifting unless their ascendants are in more stable signs because Geminis fear boredom and need to keep things fresh and interesting.

Geminis have trouble maintaining motivation because their passions ignite rapidly but wane quickly as well. They have many brilliant ideas and start projects with great enthusiasm, but they lack follow-through unless their ascendants bring greater persistence. Maintaining momentum and finishing what they start are great challenges for Geminis.

Charming

Geminis are among the most charming members of the astrological zodiac. They are good at assessing people and determining what they want to hear, which enables unscrupulous Geminis to become highly effective con artists. However, positive Geminis use their social skills to achieve beneficial goals, such as making friends and entertaining others or cheering them up as needed.

Geminis are naturally charismatic, and they tend to attract a wide circle of friends and acquaintances. They are interesting conversationalists and there is a playful aspect to their social interactions that others find appealing. They are also inclined to flatter, and people tend to like those who say nice things to them.

Gemini charm is useful when working with the public. Typical Geminis make excellent salespeople and marketers, though their talents extend to any field where being persuasive and socially adept is useful.

Geminis can enter nearly any social sphere successfully. They are good at learning the unspoken rules associated with particular groups and performing the roles required to be popular or at least accepted within them.

Social challenges are exciting rather than daunting for Geminis. Shyness and social anxiety are rare in this sign, only likely to occur if the Gemini has a more timid ascendant or moon sign.

Chatty

Geminis are the chatterboxes of the zodiac. They love the intellectual stimulation of conversation and they are good at finding topics of interest to both speakers rather than focusing solely on their own interests.

Typical Geminis make lots of phone calls, write plenty of emails, and visit many different people, often over the course of a single day. Most Geminis have a diverse collection of friends to satisfy the many sides of their ever-shifting personalities.

Some Geminis take chattiness to the extreme, talking endlessly to those who would prefer a break from the conversation. It is difficult for Geminis to restrain this impulse, as silence between two people can feel like a social failure or a breakdown of communication that makes them anxious. They want to know what other people are thinking or feeling at all times, so they have a strong need to keep the channels of communication open

Geminis want to connect with others and to know what is going on in their heads, so they pester more secretive types, trying to get them to open up. This can lead to clashes with those who prefer to keep their thoughts to themselves.

Clever

Geminis are among the cleverest signs of the zodiac. They love to learn new things and they are quick to pick up new skills.

Many Geminis have a talent for handcrafts, so they can make or repair things, though they may also gravitate to other occupations that require good hand-eye coordination. Because they are open to new technologies and quick to pick up new skills, many are good with computers and gadgets as well.

Geminis are quick thinkers, able to adapt rapidly to changing situations, incorporating new information and responding accordingly. They are good at turning changing situations to their advantage and seizing opportunities because they can assess the possibilities quickly and make fast decisions.

Geminis are also very good at discerning the feelings and motivations of others. This social cleverness can be used for good or evil, depending on the nature of the individual Gemini who wields this power.

Confident

Geminis convey confidence even when they feel insecure. They are good at self-promotion or promoting others unless their ascendants are in more reticent signs, and they tend to do well in the spotlight and under pressure.

Geminis can often do things that others fear, whether it is public speaking, flying an airplane, or some other activity that more timid individuals shy away from. This willingness to embark on risky activities stems from the confidence Geminis have in their own abilities along with their desire for excitement and novelty.

Although many Geminis have at least one area of intense insecurity, few will know about it because Geminis are good at projecting self-assurance even when they do not feel it.

Gemini confidence (or the pretense of confidence) can help them deal with difficult situations, pass challenging tests, and get hired for jobs even when they do not have the required skills or qualifications. They are good at bluffing their way through things if they need to, assuming they can pick up the necessary skills once they have landed the position.

Curious

Geminis are naturally curious. They love to learn new things, especially about other people. Some gain a reputation for nosiness because they ask intrusive questions or are overly pushy in their quest to learn about their fellow humans.

Geminis want to know what makes people tick, and many have an interest in psychology. They also want to know about the motivations and deeper feelings of those around them, why they do the things they do, and how they became the people they are today. They may pester others with probing questions or even snoop through their belongings in some cases to learn more about them.

Gemini curiosity may also be applied to inanimate objects. Some Geminis like to look inside things or take them apart to figure out how they work. Geminis who are inclined to do this will usually develop mechanical or technical aptitudes.

Deceptive

Geminis have a reputation for deceptiveness. For kinder Geminis, this manifests as a tendency to tell little white lies that make others feel better. However, negative Geminis can be quite diabolical in tricking others out of their money or getting them to do what they want them to do with a mix of lies and flattery.

Geminis will usually lie to keep themselves out of trouble. If they are facing potential consequences such other people's anger or something worse, they lie smoothly, easily, and in some cases elaborately. They are good at thinking on their feet and making something up on the spot, so they can be quite convincing when telling a whopper.

Some Geminis exaggerate significantly or lie outright just to tell a good story. They love to entertain and have a knack for performance and hyperbole, so they embellish their tales or, in some cases, make things up completely to ensure that they have a compelling tale to tell.

Distractible

Geminis have trouble maintaining their focus on a single thing. They are good at multitasking, but they find it challenging to work on a one thing exclusively and see it through to completion.

Geminis have many brilliant ideas but lack the focus required to follow through with things in most cases (unless their ascendants are in more persistent signs). As a result, they usually leave a string of unfinished projects behind them. They change their minds (and in some cases their entire lives) frequently, so hobbies and goals they were passionate about one day may be discarded the next.

Geminis start projects or activities with great enthusiasm, but they are easily distracted and lured away if something more interesting is offered (unfortunately, anything that is different from what they are currently doing will usually seem more interesting).

Geminis are great at coming up with innovative ideas, but often lack the persistence to make things happen. They are excited and motivated at the beginning stages of a new objective, but when getting down to the detail work, they will usually have a new idea and pursue that instead, leaving the last thing unfinished.

Most Geminis like to read, but they tend to do better with shorter written works such as magazine or newspaper articles. They may leave long novels unfinished or have multiple books on the go at the same time because the next book will often seem more appealing than the one they are currently slogging through.

Concentration can be challenging for Geminis, which can make studying difficult. Despite their cleverness, they may underperform academically because they have trouble maintaining focus for the time required to read textbooks and write long essays.

Easygoing

Geminis tend to be easygoing. They take last-minute changes of plan in stride and usually prefer spontaneity to rigid planning.

Geminis also tend to be forgiving of other people's annoying habits. They are not inclined to fuss and nitpick. Instead, they accept people as they are or move on if they cannot tolerate them.

Geminis can seem overly laid back to more emotional types. Their failure to get upset about many of the things that upset others can make them appear cold, unfeeling, or indifferent. However, Geminis are just not inclined to quibble over small details or take issue with mildly irritating behaviors.

Some Geminis are so easygoing that their lives become disaster areas. Their finances are chaotic, and they cannot find anything around the house because they tend to dump their belongings all over the place and forget where they put them. They may fail to get health issues checked out until they become critical or avoid dealing with dangerous situations until they become life-threating. Developing conscientiousness is a major challenge for Geminis.

Easily Bored

Geminis have low boredom thresholds and they cannot tolerate dull, unchanging situations. They are always trying new things, going out to meet new people, and even upending their lives to bring new challenges and excitement.

Geminis may move to a new place on a whim, quit their jobs before landing other employment, or impulsively jump into new relationships in their quest for excitement. They cannot tolerate stultifying routines, and they will risk everything to avoid falling into a rut.

If Geminis find themselves in dull situations or among people who are not doing or saying anything interesting, they may stir the pot and get something going just to amuse themselves. Geminis will often play with people for fun, though this is usually done in a lighthearted and non-malicious way.

Negative Geminis may provoke discord or deliberately upset others in their quest to make their romantic relationships and friendships more interesting. However, most Geminis who grow bored with others will just pester them to do something new and different to liven things up.

Emotionally Detached

Geminis live largely in their minds. More emotional types may view them as cold and calculating, but their preference for thinking things through rather than deciding based on compassion, loyalty, or blind faith stems from an intellectual orientation rather than a lack of feeling in most cases (though the small proportion of Geminis who fall into the negative category can be very cold and cruel, as they lack empathy and are not swayed by the distress of others).

Geminis are rarely convinced by emotional arguments, but most will adapt their views if someone presents factual evidence (though they may be conned by those who make things up and present them as facts). Because they are immune to emotional arguments, more sensitive types may perceive them as uncaring, but from the Gemini's perspective, a rational assessment of the situation will lead to better decision making than emotional knee-jerk reactions.

Emotional detachment underlies the ability of Geminis to make life-changing decisions on a whim. Because they are less attached to ideologies, courses of action, places, jobs, or other aspects of their lives, it is easier for them to walk away than it is for more clingy types.

Geminis can be quite insensitive to the feelings of others, making devastating remarks with little or no ill intent in most cases. They are often genuinely surprised to discover that they have upset those around them with their emotionally insensitive words or actions.

Extroverted

Geminis tend to be sociable unless their ascendants are in signs prone to introversion (Cancer, Virgo, Scorpio, Capricorn, or Pisces). Most Geminis are recharged by social interaction and love to meet new people.

Geminis are drawn to social venues where they can make new connections. Even if they get along well with their own crew of close friends, they grow bored seeing the same faces all the time and crave novelty. They seek not only new people, but also new types of social interactions and places to interact.

Geminis tend to have wide circles of friends and acquaintances. They are open to making new connections and will hang around with almost anyone, and they are willing to give most people a chance, even those who do not seem promising on first meeting.

Fickle

Geminis have a reputation for fickleness due to their constant changes of mind and preference. Their behaviors tend to be erratic and unpredictable, and they can be unreliable or unstable unless their ascendants are in more consistent signs such as Taurus, Cancer, Leo, Scorpio, or Capricorn.

Because they are easily bored, Geminis quickly go off people who provide no intellectual stimulation or challenge. This ability to walk away from those who do not excite them can make Geminis seem cold-hearted and unable to form deep relationships. However, this restlessness actually arises from Gemini's inability to tolerate anything perceived as dull or routine rather than a lack of feeling.

Geminis are quick to abandon those who fall into ruts or demand consistency. Most will also seek escape from relationships with people who are gloomy or lack a sense of humor.

Geminis are actually more likely to stay with difficult or even cruel but exciting partners or friends than kind individuals who provide no surprises or thrills. They have trouble choosing people who are good for them over those who excite them, which may cause them to overlook steady, reliable partners in favor of those who are psychologically or physically dangerous.

Flirtatious

Geminis love to get out and flirt. They often do not intend to go further with their targets, particularly when they are in exclusive romantic relationships, but they enjoy the thrill of the chase

Even Geminis who are loyal to their partners cannot resist trying to charm attractive people. This does not necessarily mean they want to be unfaithful; many Geminis are sexually loyal despite engaging in playful flirtatious exchanges, though some will take things further if they find their relationships unfulfilling.

Relationships with jealous types tend to be stormy because Geminis have trouble reining in their flirtatiousness. They do best with easygoing partners who view their flirting as a bit of lighthearted fun rather than a prelude to cheating.

Fun

One of Gemini's more appealing traits is a childlike sense of fun. Geminis are playful and mischievous. They like jokes and some enjoy playing pranks, while others like to play with language. Many Geminis have a talent for public speaking or writing.

Geminis love to try new things. They are openminded, spontaneous seekers of new experiences, which makes them fun companions for those who are similarly inclined.

The Gemini sense of fun can tip over into irresponsibility at times. When Geminis have the opportunity to do something new and exciting, they may leave necessary tasks undone, cancel plans with others at the last minute, or throw their money away to pursue a new adventure.

Geminis make great companions for those who are restless, easily bored, and afraid of falling into stultifying routines. On the other hand, they tend to clash with partners and friends who require consistency and stability in their lives.

Funny

The sign of Gemini is associated with humor, and Geminis tend to shine in this area, coming up with clever, hilarious ways of expressing things. Geminis use humor to deal with difficult situations or emotions, defuse conflict, deflect anger, and amuse themselves and others.

Gemini humor ranges from lighthearted to meanspirited, depending on the kindness of the individual. Some Geminis use humor to make others happy and entertain them, while others deliver viciously pointed, well-executed jibes to skewer those they dislike. However, this latter sort of humor is only seen in Geminis with a cruel streak. Most tend toward the playful, lighthearted side, though some of their jokes may still be a bit edgy.

Geminis have a talent for seeing the humor in even the direst situations. They are also good at laughing at themselves when they screw up, which reduces the sting of failure and allows them to gain valuable insights from situations that would otherwise be irredeemably devastating.

Generous

Geminis are generous to a fault. They love sharing a good time with others and are quick to buy a round of drinks or pick up the tab for a lavish meal. Financial carelessness combined with altruistic generosity ensures that Geminis pay for more than their fair share when the goal is fun for all.

Geminis will loan their last few dollars to a friend in need and share whatever they have with others. They live in the moment and tend not to think about the future, so they can leave themselves in terrible situations when they take care of someone else financially at their own expense.

Geminis are also generous with their time. They will happily offer their services to help a friend move (though they will probably show up late) or bring supplies to a sick family member.

Because Geminis are generous by nature, they often fail to notice when relationships become one-sided, with Gemini doing all the giving and a partner or friend doing all the taking.

Geminis do not keep track of what they do versus what others do for them, so their relationships are often asymmetrical. Kind Geminis may be taken advantage of, while selfish Geminis take advantage of generous partners and friends.

Idealistic

Geminis are very idealistic. They believe that people are basically good and can change for the better, that their own lives will improve, and that the world can be made better with the right actions. Unless their ascendants are in more cynical or suspicious signs, they tend to trust people and take them at face value, so they can be deceived by unscrupulous types.

Most Geminis assume that bad behavior is attributable to negative life experiences, particularly in childhood, rather than intrinsic badness. As a result, they tend to be forgiving of other people's lapses and give them many chances (sometimes too many).

Some Geminis are drawn to causes or volunteer work because they believe that if the right things are done for others, they will respond positively. They trust that those who are properly supported will be cured of their afflictions or addictions or steered away from bad behaviors and onto the right life track.

Because they are naturally idealistic, some Geminis are drawn to helping professions or work tirelessly on behalf of good causes as volunteers.

Impulsive

Impulsiveness is a significant problem for Geminis. On the positive side, it enables them to be spontaneous and to have interesting experiences that they would have missed if they took the time to think things through rather than leaping in heedlessly. On the other hand, impulsiveness puts Geminis at risk for many dire consequences.

Geminis rush into relationships before they have truly gotten to know the other person. They often jump from an unfulfilling relationship to something that seems more interesting, only to find they have leapt from the frying pan to the fire.

Geminis also spend their money impulsively. If they see something they want to acquire or an activity they want to engage in, or they have a generous impulse toward others, they blow their cash with little (if any) thought for the future. As a result, they can end up in terrible financial circumstances.

Geminis who are inclined toward physical risk taking also tend to be impulsive in their sporting choices. They may take needless risks by not checking gear thoroughly or placing it properly, unless their ascendants are in more conscientious signs (Taurus, Cancer, Virgo, Scorpio, or Capricorn). They may also try a new sport or other activity without thinking about the risks or whether they have the required skills to do it safely.

A small proportion of Geminis drift into criminal activity because they make choices about whether to do something illegal on impulse without thinking it through. Others impulsively decide to help people they do not know and fall for scams.

Taking the time to think things through and assess the benefits, risks, and overall wisdom of a course of action before embarking on it is a major challenge for Geminis.

Indecisive

Geminis tend to be indecisive because they are pulled in two or more directions simultaneously. Their indecisiveness is at least partially attributable to open-mindedness and idealism. Open-mindedness enables Geminis to contemplate new opportunities rather than simply rejecting anything new or different, and idealism allows them to see the positive aspects of each choice.

Geminis hate to commit themselves to a single course of action because doing so shuts off other possibilities and opportunities. They hate to shut a door on anything, preferring to keep their options open, which can make it difficult for them to settle on a single career, relationship, or place of residence.

Inquisitive

Geminis are naturally curious. They want to learn about the world around them, and they are particularly interested in what makes others tick.

Some people find Geminis nosey because they ask lots of questions and probe more secretive types for information. They want to know what is going on in other people's heads, and they will pester them or even press their buttons to get a response If they do not offer the information voluntarily.

Some Geminis even go so far as to provoke others to see how they will respond. Because Geminis are so interested in human psychology and behavior, they can aggravate those around them in their quest for understanding and insights.

On the positive side, Gemini inquisitiveness often leads to a penchant for lifelong learning. Most Geminis like to read, or they seek out educational shows, podcasts, or seminars to learn new things throughout their lives.

Intellectual

Gemini is among the signs of the zodiac that skew more toward the intellectual than the emotional. Unless their ascendants are in water signs (Cancer, Scorpio, or Pisces) or a passionate fire sign such as Leo, Geminis prefer to think about things rather than feeling their way through them.

Geminis love analyzing people, situations, movies, shows, or books, and they appreciate any conversation that gives their intellects a good workout.

Geminis may get into arguments because they enjoy the intellectual stimulation of a good debate. Some Geminis like to take a devil's advocate position or argue a side they do not actually believe in just to see how others respond and what sort of counter-arguments they come up with to defend their points of view.

Geminis have a thirst for knowledge and they require constant intellectual stimulation. They regularly pick up bits and pieces of information from a wide variety of sources, and they can converse with interest and some knowledge on most subjects.

Moody

Despite their emotional detachment, Geminis can be surprisingly moody. This problem stems largely from the fact that they are not in touch with their emotions, so they sometimes have trouble processing their emotional responses or even determining why they feel irritated or upset. They tend to think about things or talk about things rather than feeling them out, so they do not cope well with strong emotions.

Geminis are also very changeable, which affects their emotional stability. They can be happy one minute, annoyed the next, then worried, then back to cheerfulness. They often cycle through many different moods over the course of a single day (or even a single hour, in some cases).

Gemini moodiness is also partially attributable to rapidly changing desires. What makes a Gemini happy one day can make the same Gemini unhappy the next. Stable situations may actually contribute to moodiness because Geminis thrive on novelty and change.

Open-minded

Geminis are open to new ideas, points of view, ideologies, experiences, and people. They are willing to change their belief systems if new, compelling evidence is presented, and they will try almost anything once.

Geminis give new people a chance, even if they do not seem promising on first meeting, and they enjoy interacting with people who are very different from themselves and can offer an original perspective.

Gemini open-mindedness is largely a good trait, though it can be problematic because some Geminis are open to even the craziest ideas. Geminis can be drawn into crackpot schemes or bizarre ideologies because they are willing to entertain even the strangest perspectives.

Geminis are less likely to reject others for having different beliefs or lifestyles. When they reject people, it is usually because they find them boring rather than over a lack of common ground. Geminis like to spend time with people who introduce them to new ideas and activities.

Most Geminis prefer intellectually stimulating disagreement to pleasant but dull agreeability. As a result, they may spend time with people the majority consider difficult or unpleasant, and others may question their choices of friends and partners.

Optimistic

Geminis are set to sunny side up unless their ascendants incline them to be more gloomy and pessimistic. Otherwise, they rarely stay down for long.

Geminis are good at recovering from setbacks. They grieve things briefly and them move on, finding reasons to look on the bright side.

Gemini optimism provides some protection against wallowing in sadness or falling into patterns of negative rumination. However, it can also lead to overconfidence in some cases.

Geminis often start new projects, business ventures, and relationships with great enthusiasm and expectations of wild success even when there are many indicators of impending failure or disaster. Their natural optimism makes it difficult to spot red flags or imagine how things might go wrong when they are riding a wave of excitement over some new venture.

Persuasive

Geminis are persuasive speakers and writers, which gives them a talent for sales, marketing, and (for negative Geminis) manipulating others into doing what they want. Geminis can talk others into or out of anything. Whether this power is used for good or evil will depend on the ethics of the individual Gemini.

Positive Geminis can persuade others to make good choices and feel better about themselves. Many Geminis make good counsellors, life coaches, or supportive friends who have a knack for boosting others out of their depressions and encouraging them to step out of their comfort zones or do beneficial things.

Negative Geminis, on the other hand, can persuade others to part with their money or belongings or take serious risks for the Gemini's amusement. Unethical Geminis may drift into crime or shady business dealings, or use and abuse their romantic partners, applying their powers of persuasion to bend others to their will.

Unscrupulous Geminis may become scam artists because they have a natural talent for manipulating people. However, most Geminis put their communication and persuasion skills to better use, attaining success in communications and media-related industries or writing for profit, to promote charitable causes, or for personal enjoyment. Many Geminis do well in jobs where they have opportunities to interact with the public, applying their considerable powers of persuasion to charm and sway potential customers and clients.

Progressive

Typical Geminis are drawn to modern things. They follow current trends and love new gadgets unless their ascendants incline them to be more past-oriented and nostalgic, and they tend to be particularly good with technologies that facilitate communication and information transfer.

Most Geminis have modern attitudes, gravitating to progressive social views and political positions and favoring ideologies that allow for greater personal freedom. They tend to be on the cutting edge of everything from fashion to belief systems to new technology adoption (the exceptions to this rule are Geminis with rising signs or other natal zodiac elements that pull them in the direction of conservatism).

Gemini progressiveness stems largely from adaptability and a low boredom threshold. Most Geminis do not become mired in outdated beliefs and ways of living. Instead, they have the flexibility and love of novelty required to embrace positive change and seize the opportunities it offers.

Restless

Geminis are restless and quick to move on if relationships, work environments, or friendships grow routine. Many change their places of residence more often than most, in some cases changing up their romantic partners frequently as well.

It is difficult for Geminis to settle down unless they are in environments that provide plenty of novelty, excitement, challenge, and intellectual stimulation. Otherwise, they will often have their eyes on the horizon, imagining other possibilities rather than being content with their current situations.

Gemini restlessness can lead to new adventures and serendipitous experiences, but also disaster if they leave good jobs, partners, or places of residence on impulse, overturning their lives in their quest for excitement and new experiences.

Driven by whims and impulses, Gemini behavior is often erratic and unpredictable, and in some cases, nervous and hyperactive. Geminis often make snap decisions without considering the consequences or initiate sweeping life changes just to see what will happen.

Geminis never want to miss anything, and they have trouble sitting still and relaxing. They tend to be physically or mentally active at all times, and they often deprive their bodies of sleep or even food because they are too busy to allow for eight hours of rest or a proper, sit-down meal, leading to nervous exhaustion or malnutrition.

Geminis tend to flit from one thing to another, never settling for long on any given activity or career (unless their work provides plenty of novelty and excitement). They do better in jobs that require a wide variety of tasks and provide opportunities for socializing.

Typical Geminis are happier working at several different part-time or temporary jobs or projects rather than committing to one full-time occupation because they crave variety and require new experiences to maintain their interest.

Self-absorbed

Geminis can come across as self-absorbed because they spend a lot of time engaging in self-analysis. They are curious about themselves as well as other people, and because they are emotionally detached, they spend a lot of time trying to figure out why they feel what they feel and do the things they do.

Geminis also like to talk, and they often talk about themselves, though their reputation for self-absorption is usually unfair because Geminis show a lot of interest in others as well. Most Geminis are just interested in people in general, themselves included.

Geminis can also come across as self-absorbed because of their impulsiveness. If they want something or they want to do something, they tend to just go for it without taking the time to consider how their actions will affect others. As a result, they can appear uncaring and selfish, but this failure to take the feelings of others into account arises more from a tendency to live in the moment, heedless of the consequences, than from a lack of feeling for other people.

Tolerant

Geminis have a high tolerance for the quirks, idiosyncrasies, and annoying habits of others. This enables them to get along well with many different people, including those that others find irritating or even unbearable.

Geminis also tend to be tolerant of other religions, political views, and lifestyles (unless their ascendants incline them to be more narrow-minded than is typical for this sign). They rarely end friendships or refuse to consider romantic prospects based on differences of opinion.

Geminis are live-and-let-live people. They might analyze or even criticize others, but they rarely interfere with their choices (the exception to this rule is a Gemini with a more controlling ascendant or moon sign).

Geminis also have a higher-than-average tolerance for a partner's flirting (this tendency is diminished in Geminis with possessive ascendants such as Taurus, Cancer, Leo, or Scorpio). Unless they have evidence that their partners are unfaithful, Geminis are not inclined to make a fuss, and some will even forgive the odd infidelity to hang on to a relationship that gives them other things they desire.

Unreliable

Geminis have a well-deserved reputation for unreliability. Unless their ascendants are in more conscientious signs such as Taurus, Cancer, Virgo, Scorpio, or Capricorn, they miss appointments, show up late for social engagements, lose things, forget to pay bills, squander cash, or change plans at the last minute, driving more pragmatic individuals crazy.

Geminis have trouble doing anything consistently. They may promise things in a burst of enthusiasm, truly believing that they will follow through, only to lose steam and abandon a project or course of action when others are counting on them.

Lack of reliability is often a source of conflict between Geminis and their families, friends, and coworkers. Developing time-management and organizational skills as well as the ability to follow through with things are real challenges for this sign.

The Atypical Gemini

The sun sign isn't the only element that influences personality. Aspects and planetary placements, particularly the moon sign and rising sign (ascendant), are also important. For example, a Gemini with Taurus rising will be more consistent, reliable, and better with money than a typical Gemini, and with Cancer rising, a Gemini will be more sensitive to the feelings of others. Leo rising makes a Gemini more passionate, loyal, and physically affectionate; Virgo rising creates a more practical personality; and Capricorn rising can make a Gemini more secretive, diplomatic, and musically talented, whereas Pisces rising can add strong spiritual leanings or artistic talents.

There are many websites that offer free chart calculation to determine other planetary placements and aspects. Learning these other planetary placements and aspects is recommended, as it provides a more comprehensive personality profile.

See Appendix 2 for information about other astrological influences on personality.

Chapter 2: Gemini Love and Friendship Style

Geminis are unpredictable, fun, and intellectually stimulating companions. Friends and lovers appreciate Gemini's lively spontaneity, though more emotional types may find them insensitive.

Uplifting

Geminis have a great sense of humor and most are able to laugh at themselves, which can help relationships endure through rough times. They are also youthful, inquisitive, and inclined to seek new experiences, which can prevent relationships from becoming boring or predictable, and their upbeat personalities are uplifting to friends and lovers. However, their constant changes of mind and mood can make more consistent types feel insecure.

Sociable

Typical Geminis like to spend time with lots of different people to fulfill their need for novelty and diverse intellectual stimulation, and this can upset more possessive types, particularly when combined with the Gemini tendency to flirt. Ideal companions for Gemini are extroverted, not prone to jealousy, and comfortable with change.

Communicative

Geminis are talkers—they love to communicate and share, and they are curious about others. They need their friends and lovers to be very open with them and in turn, they will tell their companions everything that is on their minds. The downside to this openness is that Geminis complain a fair bit, which may put some people off. However, on the positive side, it keeps the lines of communication open so that issues are more likely to be dealt with before they become too large to resolve.

Open-minded

Because they tend to be open-minded, Geminis are almost always interesting to talk to, which can keep relationships from stagnating. They love learning and appreciate companions who have knowledge to impart and can provide intellectual stimulation. Ideally, friends and lovers will have many different interests and be open to new experiences and ideas. Geminis do best with companions who seek personal growth and transformation rather than those who require consistency and routines.

Tolerant

Geminis have many quirks and idiosyncrasies, and they tend to be very tolerant of the quirks and eccentricities of others, which makes them easy company. They can be a bit scattered, chaotic, or even unreliable at times, showing up late or missing appointments and losing or forgetting things, but they tend to forgive similar lapses in others.

Exacting, fussy, financially cautious, secretive, and uptight people make Geminis feel oppressed. Typical Geminis are happiest in romantic relationships and friendships with other independent-minded people who share their thoughts and feelings freely and do not hold grudges over small things.

Chapter 3: Gemini Compatibility with Other Sun Signs

Note: There is more to astrological compatibility than sun signs alone. Other elements in a person's natal zodiac also play a role. Ascendants (rising signs), moon signs, and other planetary placements and aspects also shape personality and affect compatibility. For example, a Gemini with Taurus rising will be more consistent and reliable, and therefore a better match for a Capricorn, and a Virgo with Gemini rising will be more compatible for someone with the sun in Gemini than a typical Virgo. For more information on other natal chart elements, see Appendix 2.

Gemini + Aries

This is a very good combination. These two can have a lot of fun together and generate plenty of creative ideas. However, it may be a light connection, lacking in passion and staying power unless other aspects of their natal zodiacs create more depth of feeling. Otherwise, this pairing is great for friendship but may lack the deeper bonding required for a romantic relationship.

Both Aries and Gemini are very good at coming up with ideas and starting new things, but they often grow bored and move on before finishing them, and this tendency can afflict their relationships. If neither individual works to keep things going through the duller phases of a relationship, both may wander off in search of new connections and experiences. However, impulsive Aries and unpredictable Gemini are less likely to bore one another than those of many other sun-sign combinations.

Aries and Gemini tend to be quite compatible in day-to-day life. Both are typically chatty, extroverted, and humorous, and they like to mix with a wide variety of people, immersing themselves fully in the social and cultural worlds (unless their ascendants are in shyer signs). Both seek new experiences and hate to get into ruts. However, despite these similarities, differences in how these two signs interact with the world can create problems.

Aries runs on feelings and instincts while Gemini is a creature of the mind. Fiery Aries may try to provoke a passionate response and become frustrated when Gemini analyses the interaction dispassionately. Aries may also grow impatient with Gemini's bouts of indecisiveness, as Aries is inclined to make snap decisions and view the inability to make quick choices as a sign of weakness. Unless Gemini is willing to let Aries take the lead, Aries will suffer continuous frustration. In addition, with two such uninhibited individuals, there is a risk that things will be said that should not be, but both signs tend to be forgiving, so fights are less likely to inflict lasting damage on the relationship.

Gemini and Aries can have a lot of fun together, whether as friends or lovers, though as business partners, they might need to bring in an additional person with more staying power. Although both signs are great at generating new ideas, they typically lack follow-through (unless they have more perseverant rising signs such as Taurus, Cancer, Virgo, Scorpio, or Capricorn).

In a romantic relationship, these two are likely to capture and maintain one another's interest. Ideally, they will balance each other out, with forceful Aries acting as the decisive anchor within the relationship to help focus Gemini's scattered energies, and mentally flexible Gemini introducing new ideas, insights, and activities to keep Aries intrigued and entertained.

Gemini + Taurus

Taurus and Gemini may be drawn together because each has something the other lacks. Gemini appreciates Taurus's stability and calm demeanour, while Taurus finds Gemini's quick wit and mental agility intellectually stimulating. However, when they spend time together on a regular basis, Taurus may find Gemini flighty and erratic, while Gemini finds Taurus too predictable.

Driven by restless energy, Geminis tend to flit from one idea or interest to the next. Tauruses, on the other hand, like to delve into things in depth and see them through to completion. Given these differing approaches, Taurus will probably be aggravated by Gemini's inability to commit to and complete what is started, while Gemini may find Taurus's rigidity oppressive.

In addition to temperamental differences, there are likely to be significant differences in preferred lifestyles with these two signs. A typical Taurus enjoys home-based pursuits, small gatherings of long-term friends, or getting out into nature (a hike in the woods, a stroll on the beach, or a picnic). A typical Gemini is more culture-focused, seeking out social gatherings where there are opportunities to talk and flirt with new people (this is another problem with this pairing; Gemini's flirtatiousness is likely to trigger Taurean possessiveness). An additional problem is that Taurus is happy to spend the whole day doing one thing, whether it is working on a project, walking through a forest, or lying on the beach with a good book, while Gemini wants to do many things for a short time each day and quickly grows bored and irritable without a constant stream of new interactions, experiences, and activities.

This is a difficult combination, but not impossible. If other elements in their natal zodiacs are compatible, this can mitigate many of the worst problems associated with the Taurus-Gemini pairing.

In a best-case scenario, Taurus will act as much-needed stabilizing force for Gemini, while Gemini prevents Taurus from becoming too routine-bound. Taurus can benefit from adopting some of Gemini's mental flexibility, while Gemini's life prospects will be vastly improved by cultivating some Taurean perseverance and reliability. Ideally, these two will pick up one another's more beneficial traits through association while diminishing their own less favorable attributes.

Gemini + Gemini

This is a fun and intellectually stimulating combination, though it may lack emotional depth unless these two have their ascendants or moons in earth or water signs.

Geminis understand one another's need for plenty of social interaction and food for thought. One of the best things about the Gemini-Gemini match is that neither individual will find the other boring, which is critical to relationship success for such a restless sign.

Two Geminis will constantly introduce each other to new ideas and activities, and there will be plenty of interesting conversation (though there may be a tendency to focus on thoughts at the expense of feelings). These two will probably have an active social life together, enriching their union with a broad circle of friends and keeping things lively with a steady stream of new hobbies and interests.

Two Geminis tend to have many things on the go at once and skip from one activity to the next, which can be a problem if they are trying to run a business or complete a project together because although they can generate an endless supply of great ideas, neither is inclined to follow through with the detail work. However, they will usually enjoy their time together.

Despite its many positive attributes, the Gemini-Gemini pairing can be problematic in some cases because there is no stable anchor in this relationship unless one or the other has a strong rising sign such as Taurus, Leo, Scorpio, or Capricorn. Without an anchor, Geminis can lead hectic, chaotic lives, making poor choices, losing things, never finishing anything they start, and getting themselves into financial and social difficulties. In a worst-case scenario, neither individual will exercise any restraint or practicality, leading to chronic financial stress and other disasters. However, other elements in their natal zodiacs may have a grounding effect, making this pair more pragmatic and sensible, and their overall compatibility is very high.

Gemini + Cancer

This is a problematic match. Cancers crave closeness and reassurance, while Geminis require the freedom to engage their intellects with a variety of activities and a broader spectrum of social scenes. While the typical Cancer enjoys spending plenty of time alone with a partner, the typical Gemini would rather mix with a wider social circle and will grow bored spending time at home. Cancer wants relationship security, but Gemini has a lighthearted approach to love (the exception to this rule is a Gemini with a more commitment-oriented rising sign such as Taurus, Cancer, Libra, Scorpio, Capricorn, or Pisces). As a result of this clash of styles, Gemini may find Cancer clingy, smothering, and oversensitive, while Cancer finds Gemini cold, insensitive, and emotionally disconnected. However, although these two individuals have very different approaches to life, if other elements in their natal zodiacs bring their temperaments into better alignment, this match will have more potential.

The main point of disconnection between Gemini and Cancer is that Cancer is emotional while Gemini is cerebral. Geminis think about things, but Cancers feel them. This can result in Cancer perceiving Gemini as heartless and indifferent, while Gemini finds Cancer's negative moods bewildering and oppressive. Another problem arises from the fact that Cancers love to nurture their partners by providing what they want and need, but Gemini's wants and needs change from one day (or hour) to the next, so Cancer will be left guessing. To make matters worse, Cancer will find it difficult to give the one thing Gemini really wants on a consistent basis: some degree of freedom and independence within the relationship.

Although it suffers from a number of weaknesses, there are also some positive aspects within the Gemini-Cancer pairing because these two individuals have complementary traits that enable them to help one another in various ways. Cancer tends to be good with the practical aspects of life (the exception to this is a Cancer with a less pragmatic ascendant), and Gemini can help Cancer lighten up a bit, applying humor to difficult situations and encouraging Cancer to think about things in a more detached manner rather than becoming upset about them. In a best-case scenario, these two will have positive effects on one another, using their differing strengths and abilities to support each other through difficult times. In a worst-case scenario, Cancer's moodiness and insecurity combined with Gemini's restless anxiety, low boredom threshold, and sharp tongue will keep this pair in a state of chronic distress.

Cancer requires sensitivity and reassurance from a partner, neither of which the typical Gemini is inclined to provide, so Cancer may suffer from a chronic bad mood, and Gemini, who tends to be the more fickle of the two, may wander off in search of a more cheerful companion.

Overall, the success of this relationship will probably depend on Gemini's sensitivity to Cancer's feelings and Cancer's willingness to let Gemini have some freedom and space to pursue friendships and interests outside the primary relationship. A Gemini in a relationship with a Cancer must learn to recognize signs of insecurity and be emotionally gentle and supportive as needed. Cancer, in turn, must allow Gemini a greater degree of independence. If these two individuals can meet one another halfway and their ascendants bring their temperaments into better alignment, this pair will have more staying power. For example, a Gemini with Taurus, Cancer, or Scorpio rising will be much more commitment-oriented, and a Cancer with Aquarius rising will be less needy and more independent (though also less stable and pragmatic).

Gemini + Leo

Gemini-Leo is a fun combination. Both individuals tend to be childlike, spontaneous, and playful, unless other elements in their natal zodiacs incline them toward seriousness. Leo's optimism and confidence soothes Gemini's anxieties, while vivacious, unpredictable Gemini holds Leo's interest and prevents things from becoming dull. Both signs tend to be friendly and sociable, so they will enjoy going out and doing things together. However, although compatibility is high with this match, there may be a few points of contention.

One issue on which these two signs don't usually see eye-to-eye is the desire for novelty. Although Leos enjoy a good adventure, in day-to-day life they tend stick with the things, ideas, activities, and people they know and like, whereas Geminis crave novelty. This can create problems when Leo remains loyal to all he or she loves while Gemini wanders off in search of something untried. This can make Leo feel insecure and jealous (particularly if Gemini's outside interests include other people), and Gemini may be irritated by Leo's possessiveness and need for attention. However, in a best-case scenario, Leo will help Gemini cultivate deeper connections with people, places, and ideas, while

Gemini will encourage Leo to try new things and seek new experiences.

In a romantic relationship, Leo might push Gemini for more commitment and personal attention than Gemini is ready or able to give and suffer insecurity in response to Gemini's emotional detachment. Leo may also be irritated by Gemini's social butterfly tendencies because Leos like to be the center of attention. To make matters worse, the infamous Leo pride may be wounded by Gemini's tendency to poke fun at others. However, despite these issues, Gemini and Leo should get along quite well in day-to-day life (unless other elements in their natal zodiacs are unfavorable) because their lifestyle preferences tend to be similar and they also have some complementary abilities that are beneficial to their relationship. Leos, with their strong organizational skills and perseverance, are better at seeing things through and dealing with the responsibilities of day-to-day life, while Geminis have a talent for keeping things fresh and interesting so that Leos don't grow bored.

This pair does suffer from a significant flaw that can create problems in business and romantic relationships: both tend to be bad with money. The typical Leo is a decadent spendthrift, and Gemini tends to be impulsive, acting in the moment with little thought for the consequences. As a result, these two may spiral into bankruptcy together unless their ascendants are in more pragmatic signs such as Cancer, Capricorn, Virgo, or Taurus. Neither is inclined to have a restraining effect on the other, so this pair will need to keep a close eye on their finances.

Gemini + Virgo

Although this is an intellectually stimulating combination, there is likely to be a lot of friction between these two. Virgo may find Gemini too inconsistent and unreliable, while Gemini finds Virgo overly cautious or critical. On the other hand, both signs are cerebral and analytical by nature, so they can have plenty of fascinating conversations and learn a lot from one another. If their ascendants and moon signs are compatible, this can be an interesting match.

Virgo and Gemini both crave food for thought and they can enjoy a wonderful intellectual rapport, but Virgos are more interested in the ways in which ideas can be practically applied, whereas Geminis entertain ideas for their own sake. Geminis tend to skip from one thing to the next without delving deeply into anything, whereas Virgos are inclined to obsessively learn all they can about particular topics. These complementary learning styles can be beneficial, if Gemini introduces Virgo to a breadth of ideas and interests and Virgo helps Gemini develop a more in-depth knowledge and understanding of things. An additional point in favor of this relationship is that both signs tend to be emotionally detached, so neither will be bothered by this trait in the other. However, because neither sign is prone to the emotional intensity that exerts a tight hold, one or the other may wander off in search of new connections if they find the relationship difficult or not entirely fulfilling.

Living together day to day can be a challenge for this pair, as they tend to favor different activities and overall lifestyles. The typical Virgo is a homebody, preferring spend time with a good book, visit with a small number of close friends, work on personal projects, tend a garden, or go for a hike, while the typical Gemini wants to get out and mingle with a broad array of people and try a variety of new activities. Geminis also tend to have a greater interest in culture, whereas Virgos are more drawn to the natural world, and Virgos thrive on routine and security, while Geminis grow restless or anxious if things get too settled and predictable.

One particularly serious problem with this pairing is that Gemini and Virgo have different ways of dealing with the practical aspects of life. Virgos keep their commitments and are very judgmental about those who don't, while Geminis tend to show up late (if at all), and although they are generous with their time and money, they are not particularly reliable unless their ascendants incline them toward greater conscientiousness. They're generous when helping out a friend in need, but they cannot always be counted on for less urgent commitments. Virgo will also be distressed by Gemini's impracticality and poor money management skills, and is likely to respond by nagging and criticizing, which will drive Gemini crazy (or out the door).

Virgo and Gemini are very different people unless their ascendants bring their temperaments into better alignment, so they may fail to appreciate one another's better qualities and become overly fixated on what they dislike in each other. In a worst-case scenario, Virgo will view Gemini as immature, superficial, and unreliable, while Gemini will find Virgo fussy, judgmental, and repressive. In a best-case scenario, these two will enjoy their strong intellectual connection and have their lifestyle needs met by engaging in outside interests while remaining loyal to one another in the ways that count. A positive aspect of this pairing is that neither sign is inclined to be jealous or possessive, so they can allow one another the freedom to engage in activities outside the primary relationship.

Gemini + Libra

This is usually a great combination unless other elements in their natal zodiacs are highly incompatible. Both signs are sociable, intellectually focused, open-minded, and friendly. They enjoy many of the same things and even when their interests diverge, they allow one another the freedom to pursue activities and friendships outside their primary relationship without assuming that encounters with others will lead to cheating (neither sign is inclined to be jealous). These two can enjoy themselves in social situations, even engaging in their penchant for flirtation without having to worry about facing a partner's wrath (unless one member of the pair has a more possessive rising sign such as Taurus, Cancer, Leo, or Scorpio).

Although they have much in common, there are some important differences between Libra and Gemini. Both like to socialize and flirt, but Libra typically prefers to do so in comfortable, luxurious surroundings, whereas Gemini doesn't care as long as there are new and interesting people to play with. Libra tends to be decadent or even lazy, whereas Gemini is a restless bundle of energy. However, these are not the sort of differences that trigger serious conflict.

Because Libras love peace and Geminis would rather analyze a situation than fight about it, strife is less likely with this pairing than with many other sun-sign combinations. Neither sign is inclined to dominate, so power struggles are also unlikely. Both individuals are tolerant, flexible, open-minded, and willing to compromise, which helps to keep things running smoothly. However, the flipside of this is that both signs can see all sides of an issue, so neither is good at making decisions. With no strong, decisive individual in the partnership, many things may be left undone or unaddressed. When Gemini and Libra pair up, there tends to be a lot of talk but little action, which can be problematic when making major life decisions or trying to run a business.

The other potential problem with this duo is that neither is particularly good with money unless their ascendants fall in more pragmatic signs such as Taurus, Virgo, Scorpio, or Capricorn. Libras don't deny themselves any of life's luxuries and Geminis live in the moment, not thinking about the future consequences of present actions. As a result, these two have a tendency to burn through their resources together and may find themselves left with nothing if they're not careful. Indecision and poor financial management may be particularly serious problems if they run a business together. However, despite these issues, the overall compatibility between these two signs tends to be high. Their intellectual rapport is great and they can have a lot of fun together.

Gemini + Scorpio

This is a difficult combination unless other aspects of their natal zodiacs are very compatible. Scorpio jealousy and possessiveness and Gemini flirtatiousness make for a combustible mix, and even if jealousy doesn't drive these two individuals apart, different lifestyle and relationship preferences can lead to problems.

Scorpios seek deep, profound connections with others. They demand loyalty from their friends and lovers, and they are naturally prone to suspicion. Geminis, by contrast, tend to skim lightly over things (including their relationships) and are adept at small talk (a form of social interaction that Scorpios hate). Although not necessarily unfaithful, Geminis like to maintain friendships outside their primary relationships and enjoy playfully flirting with others. This can trigger Scorpio's insecurities, and Gemini may become frustrated at having to restrict activities to avoid provoking Scorpio's jealousy. In a romantic relationship, Scorpio may suffer continuous distress as a result of Gemini's more casual attitude toward life and love, and Gemini may find Scorpio domineering, oppressive, and even a little frightening at times. Unless their ascendants bring their temperaments into better alignment, it will be difficult for these two to understand one another.

There are also significant differences in how these two signs interact with others. Scorpios value their privacy and are afraid of showing weakness and making themselves vulnerable. As a result, they tend to be secretive. Geminis wear their hearts on their sleeves and tend to verbally poke at others to discover what makes them tick. Gemini may grow frustrated with Scorpio's failure to open up, while Scorpio may find Gemini pushy and irritating (particularly if Gemini grows bored with the relationship and begins to provoke Scorpio for entertainment).

In a worst-case scenario, these two individuals will develop very negative opinions of one another, with Scorpio finding Gemini fickle, superficial, flighty, and immature, and Gemini finding Scorpio rigid, demanding, oppressive, and overly serious. In a best-case scenario, these two will pick up on one another's best traits, with Scorpio learning how to lighten up and let things go and Gemini developing more depth and common sense. Scorpio's strength and stability can help to focus Gemini's frenetic, scattered energies, and Gemini can help Scorpio become more open-minded and flexible, so these two may have positive effects on one another if each is open to what the other has to offer.

Despite the many problems associated with this match, each sign possesses certain traits that may hold them together. Scorpios are perseverant and they love a challenge, and Geminis grow bored when things become too settled. The passion and intensity of the Gemini-Scorpio connection may hold Gemini's interest, and the commitment-oriented, challenge-loving Scorpio is likely to hang on to relationships even when things get stormy, so if fights do occur, they are less likely to pull these two apart.

Gemini + Sagittarius

This is a playful, light-hearted combination energies, though it may be difficult for these two to form a deep and stable relationship. For friendship, fun, and intellectual stimulation, this is a good match, but it is likely to blow hot and cold when it comes romance. Neither of these signs will inspire the other to stick around for long unless their ascendants have more staying power. Also, given that these two signs are opposites, there is some potential for mutual irritation when they live together.

The success of a Gemini-Sagittarius match will depend largely on the ability of these two individuals to hold one another's interest, as they tend to be restless and easily bored. Both are drawn to new experiences, which can either pull them apart or send them off together on a series of adventures. Even when they stick together, they give one another plenty of personal freedom because neither is inclined to be possessive (unless their ascendants fall in jealousy-prone signs such as Taurus, Cancer, Leo, or Scorpio). Their interactions tend to be intellectually stimulating and they introduce one another to new ideas on a regular basis, so this is a mind-expanding combination. Both tend to be somewhat argumentative, but they also get over things quickly and rarely hold grudges, so disagreements probably won't destroy the relationship.

Neither Gemini nor Sagittarius is particularly sensible or practical, so if they want to start a business together, they should bring in a more pragmatic partner to restrain their wilder impulses and see things through. They are big-idea people, but they usually lack the perseverance required to finish what they start. Money can be a problem with this pairing because neither has any financial sense and both are inclined to squander their resources on a good time or a long shot. In addition, although both signs tend to be helpful and generous, they may find one another unreliable in times of need unless their ascendants fall in more steadfast signs.

Because Gemini and Sagittarius both crave new experiences, frequent changes of residence, career, and overall lifestyle are likely when these two live together. Life will be full of surprises and excitement, though lacking in security and stability with this pair, unless other elements in their natal zodiacs anchor them so that they don't constantly drift off in search of new horizons. This combination will have better sticking power if these individuals have their ascendants in more solid signs such as Taurus, Cancer, Leo, Scorpio, or Capricorn.

Gemini + Capricorn

This is not an auspicious combination unless other elements in their natal zodiacs are more compatible. These signs have very different preferred lifestyles and ways of relating to the world. Capricorns thrive on routine and predictability, while Geminis crave change and novelty. Capricorns tend to be dignified and hate embarrassing public scenes, whereas Geminis are verbally unrestrained (and in Capricorn's opinion, tactless). Capricorns seek financial security, while typical Geminis are impulsive spendthrifts. Capricorns tend to be cautious, which Geminis find boring. And Capricorns are reliable and demand the same, whereas Geminis tend to rank commitments based on importance and only keep the ones they feel are the most significant. As a result of these differences, Capricorns tend to find Geminis flighty and irresponsible, while Geminis view Capricorns as oppressive and dull. There is a risk that these two will develop more of a parent-child relationship than a pairing of equals, with Capricorn cast as the draconian parent and Gemini as the recalcitrant child.

Another significant problem with this match is that these two individuals value very different traits in others. Capricorns do best with stoic, strong, ambitious individuals and Geminis tend to be happiest with light-hearted, playful types. Capricorn's self-discipline and heavy seriousness can be a real downer for Gemini, and Gemini's impulsiveness and carelessness will distress or infuriate Capricorn. This relationship may be hard work for Capricorn and rather gloomy for Gemini unless their ascendants and moon signs bring their temperaments into closer alignment.

In a best-case scenario, these two will learn from one another. Gemini could benefit from adopting Capricorn's work ethic, diligence, patience, determination, will power, and thoughtfulness, and Capricorn's temperament would be improved by taking on some of Gemini's adaptability, trust, open-mindedness, and friendliness. One trait that both signs do share is a great sense of humour, though Capricorn's tends to be more cynical or dark, while Gemini's is usually lighter and more playful. Shared humor may see these two through rough times and help them make a go of it. However, there will probably be much compromise required for these two to live together harmoniously.

Gemini + Aquarius

This is a wonderful combination for compatibility. The intellectual rapport is excellent, and these two individuals tend to get along well. In a romantic pairing, this may not be a very passionate or intense combination, though it should be intellectually stimulating and harmonious. Gemini and Aquarius may part ways to pursue other interests or because the romantic connection lacks depth, but it is more likely to be an amicable parting than a hostile one. If these two do live together or get married, their relationship will probably resemble a close friendship rather than a stormy romance.

One of the most positive aspects of the Gemini-Aquarius match is that both individuals value their freedom and independence. Neither has a tendency to be jealous or possessive, so they don't hold one another back. Although they can have a lot of fun together, they can also have fun with other friends and pursue other interests without upsetting each another. Also, both signs tend to become bored if things grow routine, so neither is likely to let this happen. Additional points in favor of this relationship are that Aquarius is better able to tolerate Gemini's changeability than those of most other signs, and Gemini is less likely to be bothered by

Aquarius's emotional detachment. Both signs tend to be cerebral rather than emotional, so they are more likely to connect based on thoughts than feelings.

Both Gemini and Aquarius are full of surprises, which keeps things interesting. They welcome the unexpected and cope well with change. Conversations tend to be fascinating and these two can expand one another's horizons, introducing each other to new ideas and experiences. Both tend to be curious and sociable, and they share a love of novelty that causes them to chase new experiences and ideologies (unfortunately, this can pull them apart if their interests diverge too much). The key to success for this match will be shared interests, friendships, and viewpoints. Gemini's views are more flexible than those of Aquarius, (Aquarius tends have fixed opinions and be very stubborn about changing them), so Gemini is more likely to compromise.

Aquarians enjoy a good debate, but they are not inclined to get emotional about it, and although Geminis may stir things up a little from time to time, they don't usually start major battles within their relationships, so severe clashes between these two are unlikely. If fights do occur, both signs are inclined to get over things quickly because neither is particularly sensitive or prone to holding grudges. If Gemini and Aquarius do part ways, they are more likely to drift apart while remaining friends (or at least on friendly terms) than to burst apart in an explosion of mutual rage.

Gemini + Pisces

This is a difficult combination unless other elements in their natal zodiacs are more compatible. Sensitive Pisces requires reassurance and gentleness, and Gemini is not particularly considerate or attuned to the emotional needs of others. Gemini may find Pisces needy or clingy, while Pisces finds Gemini cold and cruel. There are likely to be a lot of misunderstandings and hurt feelings with this pairing.

On the positive side, these two signs share some common ground upon which to build a relationship. Both tend to be open-minded and creative, so there is the potential to bond over shared activities. However, these signs also share some negative traits in common, including the tendency to be restless or anxious, emotionally unstable, and unrealistic about other people and the world in general. Neither sign is likely to have a particularly soothing effect on the other in day to day life; instead, they tend to stir one another up, which keeps things interesting but can also create a lot of turmoil.

To make matters worse, as a couple these two cannot compensate for each other's weaknesses very easily because neither is pragmatic unless their ascendants fall in earth signs such as Taurus, Virgo, or Capricorn. Pisces craves security and does better with someone who can provide stability; Gemini is a maelstrom of ever-shifting feelings, preferences, and behaviors. Gemini is better able to deal with Piscean changeability than those of most other signs but may not be willing or able to support Pisces through bleak moods and periods of insecurity. Geminis tend to do better with stronger, more decisive partners because they have difficulty managing many aspects of their lives, and Pisceans want partners who look after them or partners who they can rescue and take care of (depending on the Pisces). Independent Gemini won't play either of these roles.

Gemini and Pisces also have very different ways of relating in close relationships. Geminis tend to be direct or even blunt, though they will also dissemble to avoid trouble. Pisceans are vague, evasive, and inclined toward self-deception. Each may find the other unknowable or even untrustworthy because Gemini can't get a straight answer out of Pisces and Pisces can't get the same answer twice from Gemini. In a worst-case scenario, there will be no real communication or emotional bond between these two and their unmet needs will drive them apart. In a best-case scenario, they will bond over the common ground of curiosity, creativity, and openness to new experiences and ideas.

However, the success of this relationship will depend on the ability of Pisces to toughen up emotionally and Gemini's willingness to be more careful with Piscean feelings and provide reassurance and comfort as needed.

Chapter 4: Gemini Marriage

Traditional astrological wisdom holds that Geminis are most compatible with Aries, Gemini, Leo, Libra, and Aquarius, and least compatible with Virgo, Scorpio, Capricorn, Sagittarius, and Pisces. But what do the actual marriage and divorce statistics say?

Mathematician Gunter Sachs (1998) conducted a large-scale study of sun signs, encompassing nearly one million people in Switzerland, which found statistically significant results on a number of measures including marriage and divorce. Castille (2000) conducted a similar study in France using marriage statistics collected between 1976 and 1997, which included more than six million marriages. Findings from these studies are summarized below.

* Indicates that the marriage rate difference was statistically significant. In other words, the marriage rate between the two signs was higher or lower than would occur by chance.

Gemini Men

The Sachs Study	*The Castille Study*
1. Gemini*	1. Gemini*
2. Libra	2. Aries
3. Taurus	3. Scorpio
4. Sagittarius	4. Taurus
5. Scorpio	5. Libra
6. Leo	6. Virgo
7. Aquarius	7. Aquarius
8. Pisces	8. Capricorn
9. Cancer	9. Leo
10. Capricorn	10. Cancer
11. Virgo	11. Sagittarius
12. Aries	12. Pisces*

Gemini Women

The Sachs Study	The Castille Study
1. Gemini*	1. Gemini*
2. Libra	2. Cancer
3. Aquarius	3. Taurus
4. Cancer	4. Sagittarius
5. Aries	5. Leo
6. Pisces	6. Aquarius
7. Virgo	7. Aries
8. Sagittarius	8. Scorpio
9. Leo	9. Virgo
10. Capricorn	10. Libra
11. Scorpio*	11. Capricorn
12. Taurus*	12. Pisces*

Some Notes on Marriage Rates

Sachs found that Gemini men are most likely to marry Gemini women. As for the sign Gemini men are least likely to marry, there was no statistically significant result, which suggests that Gemini men have broadminded tastes and appreciate a wider variety of personal qualities in their partners.

Gemini men most often divorce Capricorn women, but they are least likely to part from Taurus, Gemini, and Scorpio women. Some of these results are surprising, given that Taurus-Gemini is not a good romantic connection according to conventional astrological wisdom, and Gemini-Scorpio is considered an abysmal match for long-term love. Perhaps these solid, reliable signs provide some stability for the mutable, impulsive Gemini, or the excitement of passionate clashes keeps things interesting (Geminis have low boredom thresholds, so they are more likely to stay in stressful relationships than dull ones).

It is also possible that the stubbornness of Taurus and Scorpio are balanced out by Gemini open-mindedness and psychological flexibility so that Gemini keeps these fixed signs from becoming too rigid while the Taurus or

Scorpio partner provides some much-needed stability and pragmatism. Also, Scorpios love a challenge, which may help to hold some Scorpio-Gemini pairings together as well.

The higher-than-average divorce rate for Gemini men and Capricorn women is unsurprising. Capricorns often find Geminis flighty and irresponsible, while Geminis view Capricorns as over-cautious "wet blankets" who have a gloomy, suffocating effect on their sense of fun.

Castille also found that Gemini men are most likely to marry Gemini women, and that the least common marriage partners for Gemini men in France are Pisces women.

Pisces and Gemini tend to be incompatible unless other elements in their natal zodiacs increase the common ground between these two signs. Otherwise, typical Pisceans are sensitive (in many cases over-sensitive), while Geminis are often oblivious to the feelings of others (the exception to this is a Gemini whose ascendant or moon is in a water sign). However, it may actually be the similarities between the two signs that cause problems.

Gemini and Pisces can both be scattered, erratic, naive, and at times, unrealistic. Each does better with a partner who acts as a solid anchor, and neither can do this for the other unless their ascendants are in more stable signs.

As for Gemini women, Sachs found that they are most likely to marry Gemini men, but least likely to marry Tauruses and Scorpios. He also found that Gemini women part least often from Gemini men, but divorce Scorpio, Sagittarius, and Aquarius men more often than those of other signs.

The above-average divorce rate for Gemini women and Sagittarius men is unsurprising because neither of these signs has much sticking power unless their ascendants incline them to be more stable and consistent. Both are driven to seek adventures, so they are easily pulled off in new directions.

The above-average divorce rate for Gemini and Aquarius is also unsurprising despite the fundamental compatibility between these two signs, as both tend to be emotionally detached and may therefore find it difficult to establish and maintain a deeper bond unless their ascendants incline them to be more sensitive.

They also share a love of novelty and change, so they may part ways in search of new experiences.

As for the Gemini-Scorpio pairing, Gemini and Scorpio are considered incompatible by nature. However, Gemini men and Scorpio women have a below-average divorce rate, whereas Gemini women and Scorpio men have a higher-than-average divorce rate. Why do Gemini men and Scorpio women seem to have more sticking power as a pair, on average, than Scorpio men and Gemini women? It is possible that Scorpio men are more jealousy-prone and therefore less tolerant of female Geminis' friendliness toward other men. However, there are many other possibilities as well.

Like the Sachs study, the Castille study found the highest rate of marriage between Gemini women and Gemini men and the lowest rate with Pisces men.

Finding Pisces at the bottom of the Gemini women's marriage list is expected, as Pisces is considered very incompatible with Gemini unless other elements in the two natal zodiacs make it easier for this pair to understand one another and get along. Otherwise, Gemini women may find Pisces men oversensitive, needy, or clingy, while Pisces men find Gemini women selfish and uncaring. These two tend to have very different relationship preferences and requirements, and to express their love in different ways, so it is difficult (though not impossible) for them to make a go of it.

Note: Even if your partnership falls into one of the higher-than-average divorce rate categories, that doesn't mean it's doomed to failure. The sun sign is only one element in a natal zodiac that determines compatibility, and there may be other elements in your natal zodiacs that make you far more compatible than would be expected based on sun signs alone.

The Best Match for Gemini

The best match for Geminis of either gender appears to be another Gemini, while the more difficult matches include Pisces, Capricorn, and (for Gemini women) Scorpio. However, Geminis who find themselves romantically entangled with one of the less compatible signs should not despair. Plenty of marriages between supposedly incompatible signs have lasted.

It is important to keep in mind that these are statistical tendencies; this does not mean that every romance between incompatible signs is doomed. For example, out of 6,498,320 marriages in the Castille study, there were 1,029 *more* marriages between Gemini men and Gemini women than would be expected if sun signs had no effect, whereas between Gemini men and Pisces women, there were 635 *fewer* marriages than would be expected if pairings were random. However, there still were many marriages between the supposedly least compatible signs.

Astrology is complex, and there is more to compatibility than just sun signs. Two people with incompatible sun signs may have highly compatible rising signs or moon signs that can make the difference between a bad match and a good match with a bit of an "edge" that keeps things interesting.

*The methodology of the Sachs study has been criticized and it remains controversial. I have found no critiques of the Castille study thus far.

Chapter 5: Why Some Signs Are More Compatible with Gemini Than Others

Why are some astrological signs more compatible with Gemini than others? Traditional astrologers believe that signs of the same element will be the most compatible, and that fire and air signs will be more compatible with one another, as will earth and water signs, whereas fire and air are more likely to clash with earth and water. They also believe that clashes are more likely to occur among different signs of the same quality (cardinal, fixed, or mutable).

Compatibility according to traditional astrologers:

- Gemini (air, mutable) + Aries (fire, cardinal): good

- Gemini (air, mutable) + Taurus (earth, fixed): somewhat challenging

- Gemini (air, mutable) + Gemini (air, mutable): excellent

- Gemini (air, mutable) + Cancer (water, cardinal): somewhat challenging

- Gemini (air, mutable) + Leo (fire, fixed): good

- Gemini (air, mutable) + Virgo (earth, mutable): very challenging

- Gemini (air, mutable) + Libra (air, cardinal): excellent

- Gemini (air, mutable) + Scorpio (water, fixed): very challenging

- Gemini (air, mutable) + Sagittarius (fire, mutable): somewhat challenging

- Gemini (air, mutable) + Capricorn (earth, cardinal): somewhat challenging

- Gemini (air, mutable) + Aquarius (air, fixed): excellent

- Gemini (air, mutable) + Pisces (water, mutable): very challenging

Note: Two people who seem incompatible based on their sun signs may actually be far more compatible than expected because the elements and qualities of other placements in their natal zodiacs (ascendants, moon signs, etc.) are a much better match. See Appendix 2 for more information on this.

The Elements

The astrological elements are fire, earth, air, and water. Each element includes three of the twelve astrological signs.

Fire Signs: Aries, Leo, Sagittarius

Those who have a lot of planets in fire signs tend to be courageous, enterprising, and confident. Their love of excitement causes them take risks, and they are often extravagant or careless with money.

Fire people are generous to a fault, idealistic, and helpful. They are quick to anger, but also quick to forgive, and usually honest, in many cases to the point of bluntness or tactlessness.

Fire people are energetic and often athletic. They are assertive and (in some cases) aggressive or argumentative. Impulsivity can lead to poor decisions, financial disasters, and unnecessary conflict. Extroverted and easily bored, they seek attention and tend to be affectionate and friendly.

Earth Signs: Taurus, Virgo, Capricorn

Those who have many planets in earth signs tend to be responsible, reliable, and trustworthy. They can usually be counted on to provide stability and practical help, and they are loyal to their friends and not inclined to be fickle, though when someone crosses them, they can be quite ruthless in cutting that person out of their lives forever. Slow to anger but equally slow to forgive, they often hold grudges. However, they are usually reasonable and diplomatic unless severely provoked.

People whose natal zodiacs are weighted toward earth signs tend to be physically strong and have great endurance. They are inclined to achieve success through hard work, and their innate cautiousness, fear of change, and need for security keep them from making rash decisions or gambling excessively, though these traits can also cause them to miss opportunities or get into ruts. While not exceptionally innovative, they have good follow-through and are able to finish what they start.

Air Signs: Gemini, Libra, Aquarius

Those who have a lot of planets in air signs are intellectual rather than emotional, which can cause some to view them as insensitive, though they tend to be friendly and sociable. Logical, rational, and emotionally detached by nature, they can be open-minded and non-judgmental in most cases.

People whose natal zodiacs are weighted toward air signs are adaptable, mentally flexible, and easy going. They rarely blow up at others in anger-provoking situations, as they are more inclined to analyze circumstances than to react passionately. They are also easily bored and require a diverse array of social companions, hobbies, and other entertainments.

Air people usually love change and tend to be experimental and open to new experiences. Impulsivity and curiosity can cause them to make impractical decisions or squander their money.

Water Signs: Cancer, Scorpio, Pisces

Those who have many planets in water signs are highly intuitive, which enables them to discern the emotions, needs, and motivations of others. They are compassionate and inclined to care for the physically sick and the emotionally damaged, self-sacrificing on behalf of those they care for, and even in the service of strangers in some cases.

Sensitive and easily hurt, many water people develop a tough outer shell to hide their vulnerability. They are passionate in their attachments to people and prone to jealousy. Because they are idealistic, they often gloss over the faults of others, so they can be deceived by unscrupulous people.

Water people are sensual and creative. Given the right environment and opportunity, they can produce art, music, literature, or in some cases, inventions or scientific ideas that have profound effects on others.

The Qualities

The astrological qualities are fixed, cardinal, and mutable. Each category includes four of the astrological signs.

Cardinal: Aries, Cancer, Libra, Capricorn

A person with the majority of natal planets in cardinal signs will be enterprising and inclined to initiate courses of action. Cardinal people make things happen and transform situations. This can be done for the benefit or detriment of others.

Fixed: Taurus, Leo, Scorpio, Aquarius

Those who have a lot of planets in fixed signs have good follow-through. They tend to stick to a single course of action and carry out activities to their completion or conclusion. Fixed-sign people are often moody or stubborn, and they have intense reactions to things. However, they can act as stabilizing forces for others because they tend to behave in a consistent manner.

Mutable: Gemini, Virgo, Sagittarius, Pisces

Those who have the majority of their planets in mutable signs are flexible and adaptable. They accept change and adjust well to new circumstances that can throw other types off kilter. Mutable people often function better in a crisis than in a stable situation.

Chapter 6: Gemini Children

Geminis are inquisitive, experimental, lively children who get into everything and behave unpredictably. They are hard to control in some cases, though they can also be a lot of fun.

Gemini children ask more questions than the average child and they are quick to learn, both in school and at home. They are enthusiastic communicators, talking at an earlier age than most and picking up language with great speed (they also tend to be good at learning second, third, and even fourth languages). Many Gemini children are chatterboxes, and most have a great sense of humor that is evident from an early age.

Gemini children are like little monkeys, climbing all over larger things and taking smaller things apart as they try to figure out how everything works. They should be given lots to do with their hands—art supplies, building blocks, etc.—because without these things, they will quickly become bored and difficult.

Gemini children are rarely shy unless their ascendants or moon signs incline them to be timid. They are extroverted by nature and genuinely interested in other people, so they usually have no problem making friends wherever they go.

Typical Gemini children are easygoing and not inclined to brood over slights and arguments, hold grudges, or pick fights. However, they may argue because they enjoy a good debate or find it interesting to see how others respond to outrageous statements (Geminis are very curious about everything, but they have a particular interest in human psychology).

Gemini children are independent-minded. If they want to see something or get into something, they will just do it, regardless of the consequences. It is nearly impossible to stop them, as they can be very sneaky or even deceptive when attempting to get their own way or stay out of trouble.

On the positive side, Gemini children tend to be entertaining, clever, cheerful, inquisitive, and quick to pick up new skills. While their carelessness and impulsiveness can be problematic, they make up for it with their generous, helpful, tolerant, forgiving natures.

Chapter 7: Gemini Parents

Typical Gemini parents are fun-loving, adaptable, and driven to seek knowledge throughout their lives, so they can act as role models for lifelong learning. An additional strength of Gemini parents is that they tend to be very interactive, truly enjoying the time they spend playing with their children.

On the negative side, some Gemini parents are irresponsible, unreliable, or inconsistent. Fortunately, these tendencies will be mitigated or eliminated altogether if the Gemini has a more stable ascendant (though this may damp down Gemini's natural playfulness and spontaneity).

Gemini parents must try to develop a more pragmatic approach to life, and to overcome their emotional obliviousness so that they do not inadvertently hurt their children's feelings. They should also limit their controlling tendencies, which often take the form of nagging.

On the positive side, despite being inclined to find fault with little day-to-day things, Gemini parents are quick to forgive, tolerant and accepting of their children as they are, and good at finding solutions to problems. Their mental flexibility enables them to accept their children's changes throughout life rather than trying to force them to stay the same or follow a prescribed path, so they are less likely to curtail their children's independence or crush their dreams. Although they may attempt to control the little things in life, when it comes to the big, important choices, they allow their children the freedom required to develop their individuality.

Chapter 8: Gemini Health

Geminis tend to be accident-prone, with areas of particular vulnerability including the shoulders, arms, hands, fingers, and collarbone. This problem arises largely from their failure to take proper precautions and their tendency to be impulsive or hasty in everything they do.

Geminis are also vulnerable to lung ailments, so they should avoid smoking and living in regions with heavy pollution and generally poor air quality. They are prone to developing asthma, bronchitis, pneumonia, allergies, chest colds, and ear, nose, and throat infections. Because of this vulnerability, healthy living and clean air are particularly important for this sign.

Another common Gemini affliction is nervous exhaustion, caused by neglect of the body's needs.

Geminis often skimp on sleep, food, or other bodily requirements and pay the price for this later. They hate to miss out on anything and have trouble resting or quieting their minds, which can lead to physical illness or problems with anxiety. Activities that force them to slow down such as meditation, yoga routines that involve holding poses for a long time, slow breathing exercises, Thai chi, or progressive muscle relaxation can be helpful.

Chapter 9: Gemini Hobbies

Pastimes associated with the sign of Gemini include:

- board and card games
- building or fixing things
- computer programming
- concerts
- driving
- flirting
- flying planes
- handcrafts
- internet surfing
- learning new things

- listening to or making music
- parties
- playing with gadgets and electronic toys
- reading (Geminis often have many different books on the go at once)
- socializing
- taking things apart and putting them back together to figure out how they work
- talking on the phone or messaging
- videogames
- visiting people
- watching television or movies
- web design
- writing

Chapter 10: Gemini Careers

Geminis are not suited to solitary or repetitive work. The best Gemini jobs involve a wide variety of tasks or responsibilities, new experiences, and social interaction.

Geminis usually prefer working with others rather than in isolation, and most like to meet new people. A typical Gemini also needs to be on the move, perhaps driving or walking around, constantly shifting focus, or multitasking. Most Geminis like a fast, challenging pace and lots of opportunities to interact with the public and put their considerable powers of persuasion to use.

Careers that involve moving around and talking to many different people are the ones most likely to hold a Gemini's interest. Many Geminis prefer to work two or more part-time jobs rather than one full-time job, as this may be the only way to achieve the variety they need.

Geminis tend to be skilled with their hands, so hands-on crafts are often good choices. Most Geminis are talented speakers and writers as well, so any career that allows them to use these aptitudes is favored. Many Geminis are also good with technology, particularly small, handheld gadgets, so careers that make use of modern technological interfaces and gadgets are often more suitable for Geminis than jobs that involve working with the natural world.

According to traditional astrologers, Gemini careers and career fields include:

- anything in communications, public relations, or the media
- bus driver, cab driver, or chauffeur
- comedian/ entertainer
- computer programmer
- craftsperson
- DJ
- fiction writer

- fundraiser
- journalist
- lecturer
- light manual worker (carpentry, carpet laying, etc.)
- mail carrier
- pilot
- radio talk show host
- receptionist
- repairperson
- salesperson
- shop assistant
- talent scout
- teacher
- travel agent
- web designer

Note: The sun sign is only one aspect of an astrological profile. Many other factors, including rising and moon signs, play a role in personality and career preferences and aptitudes. See Appendix 2 for more information.

Chapter 11: Gemini Differences

Sachs collected a large volume of market research data for his study, and this data showed some average differences among the sun signs for certain beliefs, attitudes, interests, hobbies, activities, and preferences. The following are items for which there was a significant difference between Gemini and the sun sign average (a significantly higher or lower percentage of positive or negative responses from Geminis compared to the average for all the sun signs). Not all Geminis followed these trends; they were just more likely to match them than those of other sun signs.

Political Views

Geminis were more likely to describe themselves as liberal. With their ability to contemplate both sides of an argument, it is unsurprising that many Geminis favor moderate political positions that accommodate diversity.

Geminis do not gravitate to extremes unless other elements in their natal zodiacs override the Gemini tendency to seek balance and keep an open mind. Certain aspects and ascendant-moon combinations may pull Geminis toward the radical left or extreme right of the political spectrum, but most Geminis will be drawn to more reasonable idologies because they understand that other people have different needs and that they cannot force everyone to live as they do.

Households

Geminis were more likely to live in households with four people or more. This makes sense because Geminis tend to be sociable and like to chat. Although a Gemini with a more introverted ascendant may choose to go solo, most Geminis want plenty of opportunities for interaction built into their daily routines.

Vacations

Geminis were less likely to choose travel or holiday destinations in countries outside of Europe (the research was conducted in Europe). This suggests that many Geminis prefer to take shorter journeys for their vacations, which is in line with the traditional astrological view of Gemini as the sign associated with short journeys (long journeys fall under the rulership of Sagittarius).

Current Affairs

Geminis were more likely to read regional or daily newspapers and magazines, which is in keeping with the Gemini need to learn new things and switch topics frequently to allay boredom (when Geminis read longer books, they often have several novels on the go at once).

Sports

Geminis were less likely to play European football (soccer) than the average for the sun signs. The sign of Gemini rules over the arms and hands, so it is possible that Geminis are more often drawn to upper-body sports (volleyball, tennis, baseball, etc.) than sports that primarily emphasize lower-body fitness.

Product Testing

Geminis were keener than those of other sun signs to try new consumer products. Typical Geminis love new things and experiences, so this is also an unsurprising finding.

Clothing

Geminis were more likely to describe their clothing styles as discreet or low key, in other words, casual items in non-flashy colors. This is in keeping with the traditional characterization of Gemini as fashionable, given that higher-end fashions tend to be more understated. Geminis also like to be comfortable in their clothing, so they tend to avoid items that will be distractingly unpleasant because they are too tight or made from rough or rigid fabrics.

Homes

Geminis were far more likely to own multiple dwellings, which accords with the traditional astrological view of Geminis as having many different sides to their personalities, and having interests, preferences, and belongings associated with each of them.

Pets

Geminis were more likely to own birds, which is interesting because the sign of Gemini rules over birds and flight in general.

Eclectic Interests

Geminis had a higher-than-average likelihood of expressing interest in renovation and modernization, computers (in an era when computers were new and few people had them), large electrical appliances, films and videos, hair care and hairstyles, cooking and recipes, video recorders, and technology in general. All of these findings are in line with traditional astrological assumptions about Gemini.

Geminis enjoy doing tangible crafts (hence, the interest in renovation or cooking), love modern things (which explains their interest in modernization and technological innovations), are good with technology (as indicated by their early interest in personal computers, video recording equipment, and other gadgets), seek convenience (which is provided by large appliances), and take pride in their appearances (as demonstrated by their interest in hair care and following hair-related trends). Typical Geminis also enjoy being in the spotlight and like to explore the psychology of human relationships and behaviors, which may explain their above-average interest in film.

Broad Range of Expertise

The market research data also indicate that Geminis were more likely than most to give advice on books, films and videos, catering for guests or general hospitality, perfumes, knitting and sewing, insurance, and video recorders and other video-related technology. Overall, these findings indicate that Geminis love to give advice, which is unsurprising, as Geminis are known for chattiness, sociability, and helpfulness as well as eclectic interests.

This diverse list of interests incorporates certain themes associated with the sign of Gemini, including knowledge seeking, love of technological gadgets and modern things, a talent for handcrafts, a social nature, and a love of flirtation (hence, the interest in perfumes). The only interest that stands out as "un-Gemini" is insurance, as this sign is not known for pragmatism, though Geminis with earth or water ascendants will usually have a more cautious, practical approach to life.

Purchases

Geminis were more likely than to purchase records, cassettes, or videocassettes (this market research was conducted prior to the widespread adoption of CDs, DVDs, and subsequent digital formats). These purchasing habits are in line with the traditional characterization of Gemini as a lover of technology with a particular interest in music and film.

Geminis were also more likely to buy video equipment, dishwashers, and (in the 14 days prior to the study) fruit punch and cocoa drinks.

Geminis like gadgets and film, so it makes sense that they would want to own video cameras, and because they tend to stay very busy, they also have a need for speed and convenience, which a dishwasher provides.

Fruit nectar and cocoa drinks may appeal because they provide instant gratification (a particular Gemini weakness), or because they can be offered to guests when entertaining (typical Geminis love to socialize).

Jobs

Sachs found that Geminis were more likely to be in executive or middle management positions and less likely to work in blue-collar or white-collar professional (non-management) positions. This indicates that Geminis like to be in control and seek work situations where they will have the flexibility to govern their workflow and work environment as they see fit.

Sachs also found that Geminis were more likely to be computer scientists, journalists, general practitioner doctors, vicars, university teachers, further education teachers, and psychologists, and less likely to be farmers, bricklayers, painters, metalworkers or fitters, mechanical engineers, company owners, policemen, or kindergarten teachers.

The work statistics indicate that Geminis often prefer careers where the focus is on interaction and interpersonal skills, as well as jobs that offer variety and (in some cases) the opportunity to take short journeys. Journalists, general practitioners, vicars, and some teachers and psychologists get to interact with the public, and they also have opportunities to make short journeys over the course of their work.

Typical Geminis also have a talent for writing, which fits them for higher education teaching, journalism, or writing psychology papers. Psychology is a particularly good career field for Geminis, given their interest in human nature and behavior.

Computer scientists work with technology, a Gemini aptitude, so it is unsurprising to find that Geminis are overrepresented in this profession as well.

Farmers, bricklayers, painters, metalworkers or fitters, and mechanical engineers may work alone or engage in repetitive tasks, so these options would not meet Gemini requirements for variation, novelty, and socializing. Also, while most Geminis do not mind light manual labor, many are averse to heavy manual labor, which rules out some of these careers as well.

Being a company owner requires working at the same job indefinitely (or at least until the business is sold or goes under). Geminis get bored easily and do not like to have their mobility limited, which may reduce the appeal of entrepreneurship for some.

Police officers face the prospect of violence on a daily basis as well as following a series of strict rules and procedures. The dangers and general requirements of the profession may act as a deterrent to many Geminis.

As for early childhood education, Geminis may not find teaching kindergarten to be sufficiently intellectually stimulating. Also, because Geminis tend to be impatient, they may find it aggravating to work with large groups of small children on a regular basis.

Studies

Sachs also examined the tertiary education degrees sought by members of each sun sign group. He found that Geminis were less likely than the sun-sign average to seek further education, at least in an official capacity (Geminis like to learn, but many prefer to do so on their own so that they do not have to deal with the rules, structures, and deadlines of school).

When Geminis did pursue postsecondary qualifications, they were more likely to study business management or psychology and less likely to study pharmaceuticals.

Business management and psychology require interpersonal and communication skills, which Geminis have in abundance. Pharmaceuticals, on the other hand, require painstaking detail-oriented work, often done in solitude, which may explain why this field is less appealing to Geminis.

Crime

Sachs found that Geminis were more likely than the sun-sign average to be convicted of fraud and forgery, and less likely to be convicted of drug dealing.

Traditional astrologers have considered fraud and forgery to be Gemini crimes because Geminis are good at trickery and mimicry, and talented with their hands as well (which enables them to create false signatures). Many Geminis are also good with technology, so unscrupulous Geminis can employ it in the service of criminal activity.

Gemini is not considered an aggressive sign, so it is unsurprising that Gemini crimes tend to be nonviolent in nature (though other elements in the natal zodiac can override the Gemini's nonviolent tendencies in a few rare cases).

Drug dealing may carry a greater risk of violence than even the most criminalistic Geminis are willing to tolerate, which may explain why criminally inclined Geminis are less likely to choose this option.

Chapter 12: Gemini Stuff

The following things are associated with the sign of Gemini.

Animals: cockatoo, monkey, dolphin, butterfly, all small birds

Metal: mercury

Trees: willow, hawthorn, oak, nut-bearing trees

Plants and Herbs: mandrake, parsley, lavender, dill, lily of the valley

Foods: pomegranate, carrot, licorice, garlic, cress

Colors: blue, green, yellow

Parts of the Body: shoulders, arms, hands, fingers, upper lungs, nervous system

Gemstones: agate, aventurine, turquoise stone, citrine, emerald (May), pearl (June), alexandrite (June)

Number: 5

Places: Belgium, Wales, London, Melbourne, Plymouth, San Francisco, Versailles

Patterns or Design Motifs: complicated geometric patterns

Additional Gemini Associations

Other things associated with the sign of Gemini include:

- board games
- gadgets
- gossip publications
- magazines
- magic tricks and props
- mail/e-mail/message services
- newspapers
- phones
- playing cards
- radios
- short journeys
- sketches
- switchboards
- television
- the internet
- the media
- transportation
- video games
- written works

Appendix 1: Famous Geminis

Famous people with the sun in Gemini include:

- Al Franken
- Alexander Pope
- Alexander Pushkin
- Allen Ginsberg
- Alois Alzheimer
- Amy Schumer
- Anderson Cooper
- Andy Griffith
- Angelina Jolie
- Anna Kournikova
- Anne Frank
- Arthur Conan Doyle
- Audie Murphy
- Ban Ki-Moon
- Barbara Bush
- Barry Manilow
- Beatrice Lillie
- Benny Goodman
- Bill Moyers
- Bjorn Borg
- Bob Dylan
- Bob Hope
- Bobby Darin
- Bobcat Goldthwait
- Boris Johnson
- Boy George
- Brigham Young
- Brooke Shields
- Bruce Dern
- Cameron Boyce
- Che Guevara
- Chris Evans
- Christine Jorgensen
- Christopher Lee
- Clint Eastwood
- Cole Porter
- Colin Ferrell
- Courteney Cox
- Daniel Tosh
- Danny Elfman
- Dave Franco
- Dave Navarro

- David Rockefeller
- Dean Martin
- Don Ameche
- Donald Trump
- Douglas Fairbanks
- Dr. Ruth Westheimer
- Drew Carey
- Elizabeth Hurley
- Elizabeth May
- Errol Flynn
- F. Lee Bailey
- Francis Crick
- Frank Lloyd Wright
- Frank Oz
- Gene Wilder
- George H.W. Bush
- George W. Bush
- Geronimo
- Gladys Knight
- Harriet Beecher Stowe
- Harvey Milk
- Heidi Klum
- Helen Hunt
- Helena Bonham Carter
- Henri Rousseau
- Henry Kissinger
- Herman Wouk
- Ian Fleming
- Ian McKellen
- Ice Cube
- Iggy Azalea
- Igor Stravinsky
- Isabella Rossellini
- Isadora Duncan
- Jack Kevorkian
- Jacques Cousteau
- James Belushi
- Jamie Oliver
- Jane Seymour
- Jason Nash
- Jean-Paul Sartre
- Jefferson Davis
- Jenny Jones
- Jeremy Corbyn
- Jill Biden
- Jim Nabors
- Joan Collins

- Joan Rivers
- Joe Namath
- Joe Piscopo
- John Bonham
- John Donne
- John F. Kennedy
- John Goodman
- John Wayne
- Johnny Depp
- Josephine Baker
- Joyce Carol Oates
- Joyce Meyer
- Judy Garland
- Kanye West
- Kate Upton
- Kathleen Turner
- Kylie Minogue
- Lauren Southern
- Laurence Olivier
- Lea Thompson
- Leah Remini
- Lenny Kravitz
- Liam Neeson
- Lillian Hellman
- Lionel Richie
- Lou Gehrig
- M.C. Escher
- Macklemore
- Malcolm McDowell
- Marco Rubio
- Marilyn Monroe
- Mario Cuomo
- Mark Schultz
- Mark Wahlberg
- Marquis de Sade
- Martha Washington
- Mary-Kate & Ashley Olsen
- Masaharu Morimoto
- Maurice Sendak
- Mehmet Oz
- Mel Blanc
- Melissa Etheridge
- Michael Cera
- Michael J. Fox
- Mike Myers
- Mike Pence
- Miles Davis
- Morgan Freeman

- Mr. T
- Muammar Gaddafi
- Naomi Campbell
- Neil Patrick Harris
- Natalie Portman
- Newt Gingrich
- Nicole Kidman
- Noel Gallagher
- Notorious B.I.G. (Biggie Smalls)
- Octavia Spencer
- Pam Grier
- Pancho Villa
- Pat Boone
- Patti Labelle
- Paul Gaugin
- Paul McCartney
- Paula Abdul
- Peter Dinklage
- Prince
- Prince William
- Queen Victoria
- Raina Telgemeier
- Rachel Carson
- Ralph Waldo Emerson
- Raul Modesto Castro
- Richard Strauss
- Richard Wagner
- Rick Riordan
- Rob Ford
- Robert Bateman
- Robert Munsch
- Robert Preston
- Robert Schumann
- Roger Ebert
- Ronnie Wood
- Rosemary Clooney
- Rudy Giuliani
- Russell Brand
- Sally Ride
- Salman Rushdie
- Sam Snead
- Sandra Bernhard
- Shia Labeouf
- Stan Laurel
- Steffi Graf
- Stevie Nicks

- Suze Orman
- Suzi Quatro
- Thomas Mann
- Tim Allen
- Todd Bridges
- Tom Berenger
- Tom Jones
- Tupac Shakur
- Venus Williams
- Walt Whitman
- William Butler Yeats
- Wynonna Judd
- Xi Jinping
- Zaviera Hollander

Gemini Rising (Gemini Ascendant)

The ascendant is the mask we wear, our outer persona that we show to others. In the case of Gemini rising, the external personality will show Gemini traits, or be a blend of Gemini and the sun sign. Famous people with Gemini rising include:

- Amy Winehouse
- Barbara Mandrell
- Bruce Springsteen
- Burt Reynolds
- Charlie Sheen
- Christina Applegate
- Donovan
- Drew Barrymore
- E.E. Cummings
- Fidel Castro
- Gene Wilder
- Ginger Rogers
- Gregory Peck
- Harry Belafonte
- Hillary Clinton
- Howard Stern
- Humphrey Bogart
- Julianne Moore
- Kathy Lee Gifford
- Kelly Osbourne
- Kristen Stewart
- Lady Gaga
- Lawrence Olivier
- Michael Jackson
- Michelle Pfeiffer
- Miles Davis
- Neil Armstrong
- Oliver Reed
- Orson Welles
- Pamela Anderson
- Patsy Cline
- Peter Fonda
- Phyllis Diller
- Richard Dreyfuss
- Ricky Martin
- Rihanna
- Steffi Graf
- Timothy McVeigh
- Tony Blair

Appendix 2: Moon Signs, Ascendants (Rising Signs), and Other Planets

The natal zodiac is like a snapshot of the sky at the moment of birth. Astrologers believe that planetary placements and aspects at the time of birth influence personality and fortune. The sun, moon, and ascendant (rising sign) are the primary astrological forces, though planets also play a role.

Astrodienst (www.Astro.com) offers free chart calculation, so you can use this site to find your planetary placements and aspects and your rising sign (for the rising sign, you will need your time of birth as well as the date and place).

The Most Significant Astrological Forces

Most people know their Sun sign, which is the zodiac position of the sun at the time of birth, but few know their rising or moon signs or where their angular planets lie. In fact, the majority of people are surprised to learn that they even have these things.

Of the planetary placements, the sun, moon, and rising signs have the strongest effect on personality. The other planetary placements (positions of the planets at the time of birth) also have effects, though these are not as strong and tend to be concentrated in certain areas rather than shaping the entire personality.

The Sun Sign

The sun sign provides information about basic character and a framework for the rest of the natal zodiac. However, other elements such as the rising sign (also known as the ascendant) and moon sign affect the way the sun sign is expressed.

The Rising Sign (Ascendant)

The rising sign determines the outward expression of personality, or the way in which a person interacts with the external world. It can be described as the public persona or mask. It also indicates how an individual is likely to be perceived by others (how he or she comes across socially).

When the sun and ascendant are in the same or similar signs, a person behaves in a way that is consistent with his or her inner character. When the rising sign is very different from the sun sign, the individual is likely to be pulled in competing directions or to send out signals that don't match inner feelings, which increases the likelihood of being misunderstood by others. While such conflicts can make life difficult, they are also a source of creativity and a spur to achievement.

The Moon

The moon sign is the private persona, only seen in adulthood by those very close to the person. The moon rules over childhood and people are more likely to express their moon sign personalities when they are young. In adulthood, the moon's influence is usually hidden, relegated to the secret emotional life, though an individual may openly express the moon sign persona in times of stress or other emotional extremes.

The moon also represents the mother and other female forces in a person's life. The placement of the moon in a natal chart can indicate the types of relationships and interactions a person is likely to have with women.

Other Planets

Other planets also play a role in shaping the qualities that make up an individual. Each of the planets has a particular sphere of influence, and its effects will be determined by the sign in which the planet falls and the aspects it makes to other planets.

Mercury: all forms of mental activity and communication, including speaking and writing, the intellect, intelligence, reason, perception, memory, understanding, assimilation of information, and critical thinking

Venus: love, affection, pleasure, beauty, sex appeal, art, romantic affairs, adornment, social graces, harmony, and friendship

Mars: physical energy, will power, temper, assertiveness, boldness, competitiveness, impulsiveness, forcefulness, aggression, action, accidents, destructiveness, courage, and sex drive

Jupiter: luck and fortune, optimism, generosity, expansiveness, success, higher education, law, medicine, philosophy, abundance, and spirituality

Saturn: hard work, responsibility, character, strength of will, endurance, hard karma, difficulties, obstacles, hardship, the ability to see a task through to completion, authority, diligence, limitations, self-control, stability, patience, maturity, restriction, and realism

Uranus: progressiveness, change, originality, invention, innovation, technology, science, rebellion, revolution, sudden events and opportunities, awakenings, shocks, flashes of genius, eccentricity, unconventionality, unusual circumstances or events, independence, visionary ideas, and occult interests

Neptune: imagination, intuition, mysticism, dreams, fantasies, compassion, psychic abilities, visions, spirituality, strange events, the subconscious, repressed memories, glamour, mystery, insanity, drama, addiction, ideals, inspiration, transcendence, artistic sensibilities, and creative genius

Pluto: power, transformation, release of dormant forces, change, the subconscious, suppressed energies, death, rebirth, regeneration, sex, jealousy, passion, obsession, intensity, creation and destruction, beginnings and endings that occur simultaneously (one thing ending so that another can begin), secrets, mystery, undercurrents, precognition, personal magnetism, and extremes of personality

House Placements

House placements are a sort of fine tuning, adding some small, specific details about the ways in which various planetary placements will be expressed. The planets represent the spheres of life in which the sign traits are acted out, and the house placements are the stage or setting for these acts.

1st House: self-awareness and self-expression, outer personality, responses to outside stimuli, assertiveness, competitiveness, self-promotion, and courses of action chosen (ruled by mars)

2nd House: material possessions and attitude towards material possessions and money, ability to earn money, extensions of material wealth such as quality of food, decadence, luxury, and physical or external beauty (ruled by Venus)

3rd House: logical and practical reasoning, the intellect, agility, dexterity, curiosity, all forms of communication, all forms of media, intuition about trends and public desires or tendencies, short journeys, and siblings (ruled by Mercury)

4th House: home and hearth, domestic life, domestic chores, family, babies, comfort, the mothering instinct, food, and household items (ruled by the moon)

5th House: creative self-expression, socializing, children, early education, sports, the arts (especially the performing arts), pleasure and places of amusement, parties, social popularity, amd fame (ruled by the sun)

6th House: necessary tasks, details, health consciousness, nutrition, humility, hard work, organization, service, self-control, and sense of duty (ruled by Mercury)

7th House: relationships, friendships, marriage, all forms of partnership (business and social), harmony, balance, conflict avoidance, sense of justice, ideals, the reactions of others to our actions, what attracts us to other people (the sign at the beginning of our seventh house is often the astrological sign we find most attractive), fairness, and aesthetic sense (ruled by Venus)

8th House: legacies, shared resources, taxes, power, death, rebirth, sexuality, the dark side of life, deep psychology, personal magnetism, transformation (self-initiated or imposed by external forces), secrets or secret societies, spying, and prophetic dreaming (ruled by Pluto)

9th House: long distance travel, higher education, religion, medicine, law, animals, knowledge gained through travel and philosophical thinking, high ideals, philanthropy, luck, expansiveness, and ideas about social justice and civilization (ruled by Jupiter)

10th House: career, responsibility, honor and dishonor, perceptions of authority, relationships with authority figures, relationships with business and political power structures, responsibility, hard work, limitations, social standing, public reputation, and business (ruled by Saturn)

11th House: humanitarian endeavors, social ideals, group work, intellectual creative expression, desire to change social and political structures, contrariness, rebelliousness, invention and innovation, progressiveness, change, and personal freedom (ruled by Uranus)

12th House: the subconscious mind, self-sacrifice, intuition, miracles, secret knowledge, martyrdom, spiritual joy and sorrow, imagination, dreams, brilliance, madness, sensation-seeking, self-destruction, addiction, compassion, kindness, the ability to transcend boundaries, confusion, deception (of others and oneself), and altruism (ruled by Neptune)

Angular Planets

Angular planets are planets located along the axis – in other words, planets that fall along the line where the 12th house joins the 1st house, the 3rd house joins the 4th house, the 6th house joins the 7th house, and the 9th house joins the 10th house. Of these, the line that separates the 12th house from the 1st house and the line that separates the 9th house from the 10th house are considered the most important.

Planets that fall where the 12th house joins the 1st house will have a particularly strong effect on overall personality. Planets at this location are called rising planets, so a person with Uranus on the cusp of the 12th and 1st houses will be strong in the areas ruled over by Uranus and show traits of the sign that Uranus rules (Aquarius).

Planets located on the midheaven, which is the cusp of the 9th and 10th houses, also have a very strong effect on certain aspects of personality, particularly career aptitudes and choices. Rising and midheaven planets are some of the most important factors in a person's chart, though IC planets (those located on the cusp of the 3rd and 4th houses) and descending planets (located on the cusp of the 6th and 7th houses) can also have an effect.

The IC provides insights into the self that is seen by those closest to us, such as family, as well as our family structure.

The descendant, or cusp of the 6th and 7th houses, indicates the sorts of people we are attracted to. Theoretically, we should be most attracted to the sign of our descendant (directly opposite our ascendant).

Some astrologers believe that people who have many angular planets are more likely to become famous at some point during their lives.

Aspects

Aspects are the angles the planets formed in relation to one another at the time of a person's birth. The aspects considered most important include the conjunction, sextile, square, trine, inconjunct, and opposition.

Conjunction: A conjunction occurs when two planets are 0 degrees apart – in other words, right next to one another. This powerful aspect is often beneficial, though not always, because if the two planets involved are in negative aspect to many other planets, the conjunction can intensify the problems associated with the difficult aspects.

Planets in conjunction are working together, and their influence will have a major effect on personality. People with planets in conjunction often have one or two extremely well-developed talents or aptitudes, and many people who invent things or are responsible for medical breakthroughs have conjunctions or stelliums (more than two planets in conjunction). Having three or more planets in conjunction can indicate genius in a certain area.

Sextile: A sextile occurs when two planets are 60 degrees apart. Sextiles are beneficial aspects that create opportunities. Unlike the trine, which simply drops good fortune in a person's lap, the sextile presents opportunities in the areas ruled by the planets involved in the sextile, and it is up to the individual to seize these opportunities and make something of them.

Square: A square occurs when two planets are 90 degrees apart. Squares are stressful or challenging aspects. Having squares in a natal chart often encourages creativity and ambition, as squares bring obstacles that must be overcome and strife that inspires the individual to develop necessary strengths and use creative problem-solving abilities. Squares can promote character development because they ensure that life never becomes too easy.

Trine: Trines occur when two planets are 120 degrees apart. Trines are the most positive and harmonious aspects, bringing good fortune, ease, advantage, and luck in the areas ruled over by the planets involved in the trine.

Inconjunct (Quincunx): An inconjunct occurs when two planets are 150 degrees apart. The effects of the inconjunct are unpredictable, though often problematic.

An inconjunct can indicate stress, health problems, weaknesses, challenges, and obstacles in the personality or the environment that must be overcome. Some astrologers believe that the inconjunct (also known as a quincunx) brings the type of challenges that create wisdom.

Opposition: An opposition occurs when two planets are 180 degrees apart. Oppositions are difficult aspects that can bring discord, stress, chaos, and irritation, but like squares they tend to promote creativity, strength, and character development. It is more productive to view them as challenges rather than problems.

References

Bugler, C. (Ed.). (1992). *The Complete Handbook of Astrology*. Marshall Cavendish Ltd., Montreal.

Castille, D. (2000). *Sunny Day for a Wedding*. Les Cahiers du RAMS.

Fenton, S. (1989). *Rising Signs*. HarperCollins, London.

Heese, A. (2017). Cafe Astrology. CafeAstrology.com.

Quigley, J.M. (1975). *Astrology for Adults*. Warner Books, New York.

Rowe, P. *The Health Zodiac*. Ashgrove Press, Bath.

Sachs, G. (1998). *The Astrology File: Scientific Proof of the Link Between Star Signs and Human Behavior*. Orion Books, London.

Woolfolk, J.M. (2001). *The Only Astrology Book You'll Ever Need*. Madison Books, Lanham, MD.

Image Credits

Gemini image: PublicDomainVectors.org

All other images were found on
http://www.publicdomainfiles.com

- A pair of hearts: Mogwai
- Alianças (rings): Adassoft
- Business people silhouettes: Asrafil
- Computer, tablet, and smartphone: Agomjo
- Faces: Inky2010
- Father walking with his children: CDC/Amanda Mills
- Garlic: George Hodan
- Hands with hearts: Petr Kratochvil
- Jigsaw: Yuri1969
- Lavender: Karen Arnold
- Monkeys: George Hodan
- Night sky with moon and stars: George Hodan
- Oak tree: U.S. EPA
- Penguins: Merlin 2525
- Stethoscope: Johnny_automatic
- Young girl playing on the beach: Amanda Mills, CDC